# LOSE
## weight
### *now!*

# LOSE
# weight
## now!

Sara Rose  Nicola Graimes  Charlotte Watts

p

This is a Parragon Book
This edition published in 2005

Parragon
Queen Street House
4 Queen Street
Bath BA1 1HE, UK

Designed and produced by
THE BRIDGEWATER BOOK COMPANY

Cover design by Fiona Roberts

**Photographers** Clive Bozzard-Hill, Ian Parsons
**Home Economist** Philippa Vanstone **Illustrator** Carol Seatory
**Thanks to** Karen Heal

ISBN 1-40546-142-X

Printed in China

**Notes for readers**
Before following any of the advice given in this book we recommend
that you first check with your doctor. Pregnant women, women
planning to become pregnant, children, diabetics or people with
other medical conditions should always check with their doctor
or health care professional before embarking on any type of diet.
This book is not intended as a substitute for your doctor's or
dietician's advice and support, but should complement the advice
they give you.

This book uses metric and imperial measurements. Follow the same
units of measurement throughout; do not mix metric and imperial.
All spoon measurements are level: teaspoons are assumed to be 5 ml
and tablespoons are assumed to be 15 ml. Unless otherwise stated,
milk is assumed to be full fat, eggs and individual vegetables are
medium, and pepper is freshly ground black pepper.

The times given for each recipe are an approximate guide only.
Preparation times differ according to the techniques used by different
people and the cooking times may also vary from those given.
Optional ingredients, variations and serving suggestions have not
been included in the calculations.

# contents

# introduction

There's no doubt that the western world is in the grip of a weight crisis. If you've picked up a newspaper or turned on the television recently, you can't have failed to notice the headline stories. More than half of the adult population is either overweight or obese and the outlook for our children is even worse. We know we're overweight, which is why dieting is so popular – at any given time, six out of ten British women are trying to lose weight. But the sad fact is that 95 per cent of dieters put the weight back on, and often end up gaining even more. This book will show you how to break free from the endless cycle of weight gain and dieting for good, and achieve a slimmer, fitter body that you can maintain for life.

## Quick fixes – the road to long-term success?

The ultimate goal of any weight control programme is a slimmer, trimmer you, but how do you get there? There are hundreds of different diet plans, pills and magic potions on the market promising maximum weight loss with minimum effort. The truth is that to lose weight and keep it off, you need to make small but significant changes to your eating and activity habits, and make them for good. This book will show you what to do, but you must be prepared to put in time and effort to Lose Weight Now!

## How to use this book

It's best to read through the whole book before you start so you've got all the strategies for successful weight loss at your fingertips. You'll find out all about good nutrition and how to eat well for life, as well as what foods it might be wise to avoid. The book is full of practical tips on how to cut calories and stay on track, and there is a range of delicious, inspirational recipes to get you started.

There's also information on exercise, which is essential, not only for weight control, but also for general physical well-being. Some easy, low-impact exercises are described and there's advice on how to keep moving during your everyday life. Finally, a chapter on life after dieting offers top tips on how to stay in control, so that you don't put the weight back on, and stay looking and feeling great.

▶ **Looking good, feeling good**
The right mix of diet and exercise is the only way to ensure that you look and feel your very best.

## DO YOU NEED TO LOSE WEIGHT?

The first thing to do is to check if you really need to lose weight. One way is to assess your weight in relation to your height. This is called your Body Mass Index (BMI) and is calculated by dividing your weight in kilograms by the square of your height in metres – so someone two metres tall, weighing 80 kilos, would have a BMI of 20. This is within the normal range of 19–25; if your BMI is less than 18.5, you're underweight and may need to put some on, while a BMI of more than 25 means you are overweight. However, BMI is not always a good reflection of body fat. A very muscular person may have a high BMI because muscle weighs more than fat – even Brad Pitt can be considered overweight by this measure. Your waist measurement is another way of working out if you're carrying too much fat. If a woman has a waist of more than 35 inches and a man more than 40, she or he is at an increased risk of heart disease. But most of us don't need tape measures, scales or charts to work out whether or not we need to lose a few pounds. When your clothes start digging in, you can't fit into last year's swimsuit, or you compare how you look now with a snapshot taken a few years ago, you'll know it's time to take control!

# before you start

Diets fail for a number of reasons. These include setting yourself unrealistic goals and feeling you can't meet them; picking a diet that may be too restrictive to follow for any length of time; and trying to lose weight to please other people, rather than yourself. It may also be that you just need to learn a few strategies to help you succeed.

## The right frame of mind

First and foremost, have a good think about why you want to lose weight. Make sure you think of benefits that aren't only to do with appearance, such as the alarming statistic that obesity can reduce your life expectancy by up to nine years. Other health benefits of losing weight include being less out of breath, feeling more energetic and lowering your blood pressure. If you are overweight, losing ten per cent of your body weight will have an amazing impact on your general well-being. However, it's absolutely essential that you want to lose weight for yourself, rather than because your partner, family or friends are nagging you to go on a diet.

## Setting realistic goals

If your aim is to turn yourself into Kate Moss, you are probably setting yourself up for failure. Very few people are naturally model-thin. You are far more likely to succeed if you set yourself achievable targets, such as losing eight pounds in ten weeks (the loss of more than a pound a week is not recommended, and weight lost rapidly tends to go back on rapidly). Give yourself a really nice treat (not related to food!) when you have reached this, then set yourself another target. Experts recommend that your diet and exercise goals are SMART – which stands for Specific, Measurable, Achievable, Relevant, and Time-specific.

▼ **Eat well, keep well**

Eating well should be a pleasure and a delight. A good diet does not have to be a dull diet.

**▲ The wide, wide world**
Take a broad view of the many good reasons to watch your diet – and think about nutrition.

## Education

Think of losing weight in terms of starting to play a musical instrument or learning to type. You need to master a set of skills for weight control, including setting realistic goals, choosing and preparing the right foods (you may have to learn new ways of cooking), and maintaining your self-control when everyone around you is trying to tempt you back into bad ways.

## Motivation

Your thoughts influence every action, including what you eat and how you perceive yourself. If you always feel that you are depriving yourself while losing weight, it will be very hard to stick to a weight loss routine. However, if you think positively – for example, by recognizing that you feel so much better for eating well and becoming more active – your motivation will remain high. Decide to be someone who can make your aspirations happen, rather than talking yourself into failure. That way, you'll be set for success!

# 1 all about food

Eating healthily can help you to control your weight – it is not a quick-fix diet, but rather it will encourage natural weight loss by showing you the healthiest way to eat. It is not healthy to lose more than a pound a week and it is sure, steady weight loss that ensures that you are burning off fat reserves rather than muscle. One of the keys to success is to find a new attitude to food and eating that is not about 'dieting', but about health – giving your body what it needs, and avoiding what it does not. Food should be a pleasurable part of life and, if you eat healthily, there is the added satisfaction of knowing that you are helping yourself to lose weight.

# the truth about diets

Diets have been given much press over the last few years, as weight becomes more and more of an issue and consumption of calorific convenience foods has risen. Some diets claim enormous success, yet many people find them tricky and discouraging. Even if they lose weight initially, they find the pounds piling on again after they stop the regime. Here is a look at some of the most popular diets.

## Low carbohydrate diets

These are very popular, partly because the high meat content appeals to men. They initially allow only 15–60 g (½–2¼ oz) of carbohydrates per day and some vegetables are excluded. People are encouraged to eat proteins and fats such as eggs, meat and cheese, the principle being that carbohydrates lead to raised insulin levels, under which fat cannot be broken down.

Only fat and protein signal enzymes in the body that let us know when we are full; therefore carbohydrates do not fill us up. Carbohydrates are also broken down and pass through the gut much more quickly, which is why you can be hungry so soon after eating them. This explains why many people on a low carbohydrate diet end up eating fewer calories, even though fats and proteins have more calories per gram consumed.

Of course, cutting out a major food group can rob you of vitamins and minerals, such as the B vitamins in grains. This can lead to a reduction in energy and therefore less motivation to exercise. Many people also have great difficulty digesting fats and proteins at this level, and high protein foods are acidic, which can lead to liver and kidney problems. Cutting down fibre can also lead to constipation and reduce the elimination of toxins from the bowel.

The reason this diet works for so many people is that they cut out a food to which they have an intolerance, such as wheat. Many

▲ **Be informed**
Always keep up-to-date with the latest information about which foods are healthy.

▶ **The right stuff**
Eat plenty of foods containing vital vitamins and minerals.

people have difficulty digesting wheat and gain weight as a consequence. The diet also helps to keep blood sugar levels steady, which provides energy and reduces food cravings. There are, however, other ways of achieving this, which we shall look at later.

## Very low calorie diets

These diets assume that there is a very simple conversion from how many calories you eat to how many you expend through activity. The principle is that if you eat less than the daily required amount of 1950 calories for a woman and 2550 for a man, then you must burn off excess fat. However, if you eat much less than this, the body assumes that you are going through a period when there is little food available, and slows down the metabolic rate to conserve stores. This is why people who go on crash diets can have weight fluctuations. Foods with the same calorific value can also have a completely different effect on weight: the oils in fish, for example, are used up by the brain and therefore there is no excess to be stored as fat. It is 'empty calories' – those from foods with little nutritional value – that are the problem. These are stored as fat if not burnt off.

## Food combining diets

The main goal of food combining diets is to separate your digestion of proteins from your digestion of carbohydrates. People with digestive problems can find these diets very useful, and they have proved successful for weight loss, too. It is not yet wholly understood why this is, though these diets can be tricky to adhere to, and many people simply eat less food as a result. The principle is that different types of food require different enzymes to be broken down in the stomach and small intestine, and there is less work for the body to do if only one set is in operation at a time. Good digestion is an important part of weight loss, as the proper absorption of food and nutrients satisfies the appetite. Constipation can stop the elimination of toxins, which are then re-absorbed, causing the body to hold on to fluids to protect itself. However, protein slows down the release of sugar into the bloodstream, so eating carbohydrates without protein can lead to raised blood sugar levels and sugar being stored as fat.

## Low fat diets

Devised on the premise that 'all fats are bad', this idea was popular several decades ago, but has since been modified. Weight loss results from avoiding foods that are high in saturated fat, especially those that combine this type of animal-derived fat with sugar. This is why foods like crisps, pastries and biscuits cause weight gain. However, avoiding all fats starves the body of beneficial fats from fish and plant sources. This can affect hormone balance and the body's ability to regulate fats and cholesterol, both of which can lead to weight gain. Also, many low-fat products replace fats and oils with sugar and additives that can raise blood sugar levels – the main culprit for weight gain.

## Points systems

There are many slimming clubs that provide a specific points score for foods based on calorie, fat and fibre content. A daily limit of points is set and it is up to you which foods you choose. The support group aspect of these clubs works well to motivate people, and sensible, gradual weight loss is encouraged. However, no foods are banned, so some people may use their points up on unhealthy foods, with weight loss occurring simply on account of a lower calorie intake. These people's metabolisms may slow down to conserve energy and they are likely to gain weight after stopping the system. Certain healthy foods may also be avoided because they have high point scores, such as nuts, seeds and avocados. These foods contain beneficial fats, which is why they have the high scores, but they are vital to a healthy diet.

▲ **Weight for it**
Do not obsess over weighing yourself – once a week is fine. Focus instead on how you are feeling.

# Ideal weight ranges

The table below is an indication of acceptable weight ranges for given heights. This is a general guide, which does not take into consideration that muscle weighs more than fat. If you are concerned, consult your doctor to check if your weight is in a risk category, or if you are a good weight for your height and should not lose much if any at all.

| HEIGHT–WEIGHT TABLE | | | | | | | |
|---|---|---|---|---|---|---|---|
| Height | | Women | | | Men | | |
| cm | feet & inches | kg | pounds | stones & pounds | kg | pounds | stones & pounds |
| 152 | 5′0″ | 47–62 | 104–137 | 7.6–9.11 | – | – | – |
| 155 | 5′1″ | 48–64 | 106–140 | 7.8–10.0 | – | – | – |
| 158 | 5′2″ | 49–65 | 108–143 | 7.10–10.3 | 58–68 | 128–150 | 9.2–10.10 |
| 160 | 5′3″ | 50–67 | 111–147 | 7.13–10.7 | 59–69 | 130–153 | 9.4–10.13 |
| 163 | 5′4″ | 52–69 | 114–151 | 8.2–10.11 | 60–71 | 132–156 | 9.6–11.2 |
| 165 | 5′5″ | 53–70 | 117–155 | 8.5–11.1 | 61–73 | 134–160 | 9.8–11.6 |
| 168 | 5′6″ | 54–72 | 120–159 | 8.8–11.5 | 62–74 | 136–164 | 9.10–11.10 |
| 170 | 5′7″ | 56–74 | 123–163 | 8.11–11.9 | 63–76 | 138–168 | 9.12–12.0 |
| 173 | 5′8″ | 57–76 | 126–167 | 9.0–11.13 | 64–78 | 140–172 | 10.0–12.4 |
| 175 | 5′9″ | 59–77 | 129–170 | 9.3–12.2 | 64–80 | 142–176 | 10.2–12.8 |
| 178 | 5′10″ | 60–79 | 132–173 | 9.6–12.5 | 65–82 | 144–180 | 10.4–12.12 |
| 180 | 5′11″ | 61–80 | 135–176 | 9.9–12.8 | 66–84 | 146–184 | 10.6–13.2 |
| 183 | 6′0″ | 63–81 | 138–179 | 9.12–12.11 | 68–85 | 149–188 | 10.9–13.6 |
| 185 | 6′1″ | – | – | – | 69–87 | 152–192 | 10.12–13.10 |
| 188 | 6′2″ | – | – | – | 70–89 | 155–197 | 11.1–14.1 |
| 191 | 6′3″ | – | – | – | 72–92 | 158–202 | 11.4–14.6 |

Source: based on Metropolitan Life Insurance Company tables (1983). Note height allows for shoes with 1 inch heels and weight allows for clothing weighing 1.4 kg (3 pounds).

# nutrition through life

On the whole, people become less physically active the older they get. This means that their calorific needs are less, and that they should eat less food. It is never a good idea to eat too few calories, however, as eating actually raises the metabolic rate to burn it off as fuel. Skipping meals is a very bad idea, too, as it slows down the metabolism and can cause you to eat more at the next meal. It is true that what you don't burn you can store as fat, but if the food is healthy and nutrient-dense, it will be used up for needs other than fuel, such as structure, brain function, the production of hormones and antibodies, skin healing, neurotransmitters, and as anti-inflammatory agents. Good food, little and often, can keep your body at its most efficient, and will sustain blood sugar levels and energy production. This will keep cravings at bay and encourage exercise.

We all have a basal metabolic rate (BMR), which is the number of calories your body burns each day just to stay alive. Many calorie-burning activities go unseen, such as heart function, detoxification, tissue repair and healing, maintaining the structure of bones and teeth, digestion and immune function.

Many women find that they put on weight during and after the menopause and become more pear-shaped. This is because of declining oestrogen and progesterone levels. It is important to remember that after the ovaries stop producing oestrogen, the body's main source of oestrogen is fat cells, which emphasizes the importance of including beneficial fats in the diet. Fat cells do not produce progesterone, however, and weight gain on the hips, bottom and thighs can occur when the ratio of oestrogen to progesterone is too high. Increasing exercise and avoiding sugar, refined carbohydrates (like biscuits and white bread), stimulants like tea and coffee, as well as reducing meat and dairy intake and eating more wholefoods such as brown rice, beans and pulses can help with the removal of excess oestrogen and restore balance.

## Your relationship with food

For many, eating is a negative coping pattern that suppresses emotions, such as stress, anger, anxiety, boredom, sadness and loneliness. This comfort eating can begin as a response to a single

▶ **Enjoy your food**
Nothing is more satisfying than eating tasty food that you know is doing you good.

stressful event and eventually become a habit that gets you through day-to-day stresses. Unfortunately, it sets up a cycle of eating, not as a response to hunger, but as a distraction from unpleasant feelings.

There is also a physical mechanism at work. When we eat comfort foods, often refined carbohydrates such as chocolate, crisps and biscuits, we set up a pattern of fluctuating blood sugar levels. This can affect the production of serotonin, the brain chemical that regulates mood. Low serotonin levels can lead to cravings for carbohydrates, a vicious circle that can lead to weight gain. For many, this is worse in the winter, when less sunlight leads to a decrease in natural serotonin. Seasonal Affective Disorder is often linked to weight gain.

## Inherited eating patterns

In western society, we tend to swing between continual attempts to diet or eat less in everyday life, and going completely overboard on holidays, at Christmas and at family events. It is interesting to think that Christmas was originally a feast at which healthy foods were eaten to prepare the immune system for the harshness of the winter ahead. It is certainly not so now.

Big portion sizes, always having dessert, keeping fattening snacks in the house, unhealthy diets and insisting on finishing an enormous plate of food we do not necessarily want, are all habits learnt as children that can follow us into adulthood. These patterns are not set in stone, and establishing a new relationship with food is the first step to making lasting changes.

We must also consider how our eating patterns are shaped by our parents' attitudes to food. Were certain foods withheld, and does this now make you want to eat what you want when you want? Or was food used as a symbol of love and affection that you now associate with comfort and security? If you suspect that your relationship with food is rooted in such psychological issues, then you should seek professional advice to help you break patterns that may be holding you back in achieving your preferred weight.

▲ **Good enough to eat**
How you present your food is just as important as how good it tastes.

# optimum nutrition

'Optimum nutrition' means getting the best nutrients possible from your food and avoiding 'empty calories'. This ensures that your body receives what it needs for all systems to function optimally and for it to manage weight naturally.

## MACRONUTRIENTS

These are the larger molecules that provide fuel and structure for your body. It's important to eat sources of these that also provide the most micronutrients, in order to maximize nutritional value.

## Carbohydrates

These are made up of glucose molecules that, when digested, break down into sugars that we use as our main source of fuel. If carbohydrates are broken down too quickly, we experience a sharp rise in blood sugar, which is then converted and stored as fat, being dangerous to remain in the bloodstream. Foods that contain these simple sugars are traditionally very sweet, such as fizzy drinks, cakes, biscuits, honey and chocolate. Many people crave these when they get a dip in their blood sugar.

Switching to complex carbohydrates, which take longer to digest, can lead to more sustained blood sugar levels. Good sources of these include the wholegrains in brown bread, brown rice, oats and rye, vegetables, beans, pulses and darker fruits such as berries, plums and cherries, and crisp, green apples, which all release their sugars slowly. These foods also provide fibre, which cleans out toxins, and have plenty of nutrients that are crucial to weight loss. Limit your intake of very sweet fruits like grapes and bananas, and of fruit juice, which is very high in sugar.

▼ **Bake your own**
The less processed your food, the more you know about its ingredients.

## Proteins

These form the structures in our organs, antibodies, hormones and neurotransmitters. We can also burn proteins for fuel, if absolutely necessary, although there is a risk that you will also burn muscle. Proteins are very good for blood sugar management and can slow down the release of sugar into the bloodstream when eaten with carbohydrates. They can also speed up metabolism, but should be eaten within reasonable limits to avoid excess acidity, which encourages weight gain. They are a good breakfast food as they ensure sustained energy throughout the day. Meat, fish and eggs provide the densest sources, but proteins are also found in brown rice, beans, pulses, nuts, seeds and dense vegetables like broccoli and asparagus. Generally, proteins should make up 30 per cent of your daily calorie intake.

## Fats

These are essential to make steroid hormones, HDL cholesterol ('good' cholesterol) and all cell membranes. Fats also make up the majority of our brains. Saturated fats are generally found in animal products, and although we can handle them in small amounts, they can offset beneficial fats and lead to weight gain when eaten with carbohydrates. Oils are generally beneficial when not overprocessed (avoid hydrogenated fats or oils). Oily fish (salmon, mackerel, tuna and sardines) contain omega-3 oils, which help the body to produce serotonin. Nuts, seeds and their oils contain omega-6 oils, which help to regulate blood sugar. Monounsaturated oils are found in nuts, peanuts, avocados and olives, and their oils; they contain oleic acid, which helps to regulate cholesterol and helps the body to deal with fats.

## MICRONUTRIENTS

As the name suggests, these are smaller, but no way less important than macronutrients. We shall look at those that are termed essential, which means that we must eat them every day because we cannot make them in our bodies.

## Vitamins

These are chemicals that enable enzyme reactions to happen in your body. They are separated into two categories:

Water-soluble vitamins are not easily stored and we need to eat them often: at least 500 mg of vitamin C is needed daily. It is vital for hormone production and the clearance from the liver of toxins that can add to weight gain. Good sources are berries, citrus fruits and vegetables, especially broccoli, peppers and asparagus.

**▲ Be fruitful**
Make sure you eat at at least five portions of fruit or veg each day.

B vitamins are important for weight loss and are lost in foods that are processed. They enable us to produce energy, regulate mood and deal with stress. They are found in meat, fish, wholegrains, vegetables, beans and pulses.

The fat-soluble vitamins are transported around the body in oils and fats, and work in fatty areas like the heart, liver, skin and eyes, where they protect the organ from damage. They include vitamin A, vitamin E and the carotenoids, and are found in brightly coloured fruit and vegetables, nuts, seeds and fish.

## Minerals

Every living cell on the planet depends on minerals from the rocks that make up the earth and get into our systems via the soil. Poor mineral status is a common underlying cause of weight gain.

Bulk minerals are needed in large amounts, most notably calcium and magnesium (from green leafy vegetables, nuts, seeds and fish), which work closely together in the body and regulate heart function, fluid balance and muscular activity. Trace minerals are needed in smaller amounts, but are still essential. Particularly important for weight loss is zinc, which has the most uses in the body, including blood sugar balance and serotonin production, and is found in nuts, seeds, fish, pulses and legumes.

## Antioxidants

These are the vitamins A, C and E, the carotenoids and the minerals zinc and selenium (found in brazil nuts, seafood and wholegrains). They are important in the weight loss process, protecting the body as you burn off fat. There are also natural plant chemicals with antioxidant properties, such as the cyanidins found in red, blue and purple fruits, and lycopene, which is found in tomatoes, watermelon and pink grapefruit.

The greater the variety of fruits and vegetables that you eat, the more nutrients you will receive. The World Health Organization recommends at least five portions a day. One portion is roughly a palmful, one whole larger fruit or several small ones such as plums. It is best to meet this target with raw fruits and vegetables, and to limit the intake of fruit juice, diluting this where feasible.

▼ **Variety is the spice of life**
The more varied and colourful your choice of fruit and veg, the more nutrients you will be eating.

# water and the importance of fluids

Your body's make-up is 70 per cent water and it likes to stay that way. Vast amounts of water are used daily to maintain most of your bodily functions and to get toxins completely out of your body, rather than being re-absorbed and recirculated. Signs of dehydration include dry skin, headaches, constipation and hard stools, poor concentration and bloating. As with weight gain, if the body feels 'starved' of water, then it will hold on to the little it has, which can lead to water retention.

Water is lost through the bowels, urine and sweat and needs to be continually replaced. The average requirement is eight glasses a day. You can also help to make this up with non-caffeinated teas and diluted fruit juices. Like everything, balance is important and there is a level at which anything becomes toxic. Drinking five times this amount of water has been shown to be dangerous.

If you are very dehydrated, build up your water intake slowly or you can shock the body. Diluting apple juice with the same amount of water can help to get water into your cells, but be careful not to drink too much as it is high in sugar.

Water is important for weight loss as it promotes the removal of toxins and acts as a temperature regulator. It assists in the function of enzymes and proteins, which work better diluted, and helps the body to reach its optimum fat-burning function.

## Caffeine

Caffeine, found in coffee, tea, cocoa, chocolate, green tea and cola drinks, is dehydrating. This is because it has a toxic effect on the nervous system, and the body uses up water when eliminating it through the kidneys. It is also a diuretic, meaning that it causes excess urination and water loss. Any caffeine you drink increases your need for water to replace what is lost. Caffeine is counter-productive in weight loss because it is a stimulant, causing adrenalin to be produced, with a subsequent rise in blood sugar.

A large coffee bought in a café can have as much as several hundred milligrams of caffeine, while a brewed filter coffee may contain 100 mg. A cup of tea made with a tea bag has an average of 40 mg, but of course this depends on how long it is brewed. Green tea can be very useful for helping to reduce and give up caffeine. It contains just 4 mg per cup (even decaf tea contains 3 mg) but, unlike black tea, does not overstimulate. That small amount of caffeine can be enough to ward off your craving, which is unfortunately a sign of caffeine withdrawal. Weaning yourself off caffeine completely takes three days of avoidance, but be prepared for side effects and stick with it.

## Alcohol

Alcohol should be completely avoided on the 14-day diet plan (see page 26). It contains calories with no nutritional value and depletes the body of B vitamins, vitamin C, magnesium and zinc, thus making blood sugar control more difficult. Alcohol is also loaded with sugar. This causes an immediate stimulatory action, although it is ultimately a depressive drug. Like sugar, alcohol can be rapidly turned to fat by insulin, the hormone responsible for blood sugar control. This fat is deposited in the body and stored in the liver, which it may damage. When blood sugar levels are low, alcohol is often used to raise them, setting off another vicious circle. The ethanol that causes intoxication is toxic to the body and damages all the liver's detoxification pathways. Good liver function – achieved through a 'clean' diet, with plenty of fibre and little or no sugar – is crucial to weight loss.

◀ **Water for life**
Always keep some water handy and make a note of how much you are drinking.

# a diet that works

### get ready to lose weight

This 14-day diet plan is an example of a healthy eating regime that is designed to allow you to make long-lasting changes and lose weight naturally, steadily and safely. It is not about seeking a quick fix, but about realizing what makes you feel better about your body and health to motivate you to form new habits.

The foods mentioned in this chapter are cupboard essentials, so you are always prepared to eat something healthy. Organization helps you to set up healthy eating patterns and is satisfying in itself. The 14-day diet plan is carefully constructed to provide you with a nutrient-rich diet containing the ideal amount of calories, following the principles of healthy eating set out in this book.

# the 14-day programme

'Breakfast like a king, lunch like a prince and dine like a pauper' is the best rule to live by when it comes to maintaining energy levels. It also encourages natural weight loss because you use up your energy more efficiently during the day. At breakfast, including a protein source can maintain blood sugar balance by providing a sustainable energy source; this can help to reduce cravings. Porridge oats are an alternative quick, easy breakfast. Try to make lunch your main meal of the day when possible and eat dinner no later than 7.30 pm.

Snacking keeps your blood sugar steady, as long the snack is something like fruit, oatcakes, raw almonds, vegetable sticks, hummus or tahini. Bio-yogurts with real fruit are good, as are smoothies if they have no added sugar and especially if they contain dark fruits or berries. Try a taste test with healthy snack bars and buy those with the least sugar. Radishes are a good snack food as they improve thyroid function which helps weight loss.

The amount and variety of vegetables most people eat are sadly lacking. Find ways to eat vegetables that appeal to you. Herbs, spices, olive oil, lemon juice, sunflower, pumpkin and sesame seeds, horseradish sauce, wholegrain mustard, soy sauce, pesto and tahini all add flavour. If you have had a sweet palate for years, then changing that to appreciate the taste of vegetables, herbs and spices can take time, but will gradually happen as you wean yourself off sugar. Eating zinc foods such as nuts, seeds and fish can help increase your sense of taste.

## How to follow the programme

Firstly, read the programme thoroughly and make a list of foods that you will need to buy. Sticking to a diet always involves forward planning and this also makes you feel more in control. If you are particularly busy on one day and find the plan difficult, do not feel guilty for deviating, but get back on track as soon as you are able. You can swap a day that seems to fit in with your schedule better and use examples of ingredients to make informed, healthier choices when eating out or buying something pre-prepared because of time restraints.

Try to set aside time to do the diet so that you are not fighting against it and feeling frustrated. Concentrating on looking after yourself and making important changes in your life should be given time and priority, especially getting used to new habits, shopping choices and foods. You will find out over the 14 days which recipes suit your lifestyle and tastes. Learn to listen to your body and note what it reacts to (in good and bad ways) to gain an understanding of how best to continue after the 14 days are finished. You may want to repeat the diet, especially if you feel more reassured when you have specific dietary guidelines to follow.

If you fall off the wagon, do not be too harsh on yourself, but take the opportunity to note how, although the foods you were tempted by made you feel better in the short term, their effect was negative in the long term.

## Carb-curbing

Some people find that they have more success if they limit their intake of starchy carbohydrates such as rice, pasta and bread in the evening because it is more likely to be stored as fat if not used for energy. The 14-day diet only includes small portions of carbohydrate in the evening, or none at all. Replace with bulky vegetables such as broccoli and cauliflower. Raw almonds are good for stopping carb cravings, as are foods high in tryptophan (from which serotonin is produced), such as poultry, oily fish (buy in cans for snacks on rye crackers), oatcakes, nuts and seeds.

▲ **Get organized**
Planning your meals helps you to feel in control and meet your goals.

◀ **Big breakfast**
Cereals release energy slowly during the day and limit cravings.

# the programme

The following is a 14-day diary outlining recipes in this book, other meal suggestions and snacks to start you on the road to natural, healthy weight loss. It is best to start on a Saturday so you have the weekend to get used to the changes and shop for foods. You can have the breakfast in already and then spend Saturday morning making up your shopping list and buying in the other foods. Recipes included in this book are highlighted in capital letters.

### Day One – Saturday
**Breakfast** Poached eggs on rye bread – can add spinach to make eggs Florentine.

**Lunch** TABBOULEH.

**Dinner** GRIDDLED VENISON WITH ORANGE SALSA – have as many vegetables as you can to start your new habit of using them to fill you up.

**Snack** DETOX JUICE – have this mid-morning or after shopping, and always drink fresh.

▼ **Sweet treat**
A Strawberry & Peach Smoothie in the afternoon is a relaxing treat.

### Day Two – Sunday
**Breakfast** Poached eggs, sugar-free beans, grilled, lean organic bacon and tomato – a healthy alternative to the fried breakfast.

**Lunch** CARROT & RED LENTIL SOUP – soups can be made at the weekend and stored or even frozen for midweek lunches and snacks.

**Dinner** Try a less calorific roast dinner without the roast potatoes and parsnips, which release their sugars very quickly and contain lots of fat and carbs – the worst combination. Choose a lean chicken breast with plenty of veg and boil just a few new potatoes in their skins.

**Snack** STRAWBERRY & PEACH SMOOTHIE – a Sunday afternoon treat, which will satisfy any sweet cravings.

## Day Three – Monday

**Breakfast** Always have breakfast. If you are usually rushed, just get up 15 minutes earlier. Find a non-processed, good quality wholegrain cereal that you like. If you suffer from digestive or skin problems, headaches or bloating, decrease or avoid wheat and see if this helps.

**Lunch** THAI CHICKEN BROTH.

**Dinner** GLAZED SALMON FILLET WITH ASPARAGUS or TERIYAKI TOFU & VEGETABLE STIR-FRY.

**Snack** Snack on raw almonds to beat any sugar cravings, especially those that have you reaching for sweet foods or caffeine around 4 pm.

## Day Four – Tuesday

**Breakfast** Variety is important at breakfast to ensure you get a full spread of nutrients and do not encourage food intolerances. Try porridge for some days during the week, with different toppings such as berries (which can be added directly to the hot porridge from the frozen bags found in supermarkets), raw nuts and seeds. Do not sweeten with sugar, but apple juice or a small amount of honey is fine.

**Lunch** Make a salad with boiled eggs, capers, green beans and a large leafy salad bag. These bags are always useful for making a quick meal and can even be snacked on like a bag of crisps – you will be surprised at how much energy green foods can give you!

**Dinner** ITALIAN BEAN & PASTA SOUP – if you have eaten a big lunch and kept up your blood sugar during the day by snacking on healthy foods, then it is easier to have dinner 'like a pauper'.

**Snack** STRAWBERRY & PEACH SMOOTHIE.

▲ **Keep it simple**
Healthy and attractive meals can be easy to prepare.

## Day Five – Wednesday

**Breakfast** Try a different cereal, and add a topping, like one of the porridge toppings mentioned for Day Four, or some bio yogurt.

**Lunch** FRESH TUNA NIÇOISE – get used to knocking this classic up quickly or preparing it for work the night before as it travels well. You can play around with the ingredients for variety.

**Dinner** PASTA WITH ITALIAN MEATBALLS IN TOMATO SAUCE – again, try to eat no later than 7.30 pm, especially as this meal contains pasta. A tempting vegetarian alternative is the MUSHROOM, BEAN & SPINACH TOWER.

**Snack** Always keep apples with you as a fantastic, energy-releasing food that will satisfy your sweet palate. They also help rid the body of toxins that can keep the body holding onto weight.

## Day Six – Thursday

**Breakfast** Fresh fruit salad will give you a refreshing start to the day.

**Lunch** ROASTED RED ONION, AVOCADO & SPINACH SALAD – if you need, you can add some cold brown basmati rice as a good source of complex carbohydrates, B vitamins and fibre to keep you going through the day.

**Dinner** ORIENTAL FISH PARCELS.

**Snack** Try raw radishes.

## Day Seven – Friday

**Breakfast** Choice of any from last week.

**Lunch** Make up a salad with tinned sardines or mackerel, avocado, lettuce, watercress and your favourite other salad items. Grated carrot and courgette make refreshing salad-bulkers.

▲ **Menu for change**
Ringing the changes with a range of exciting dishes helps to keep you motivated.

**Dinner** CHILLI CHICKEN WITH CHICKPEA MASH – a tasty treat that can be shared with friends at a dinner party.

**Snack** Children's fruit bar or health bar (check sugar content).

## Day Eight – Saturday

**Breakfast** Smoked mackerel or haddock with poached eggs and rye bread.

**Lunch** SESAME PRAWN NOODLE SALAD.

**Dinner** TABBOULEH – good to keep as a snack, it can always be added as a side dish to meals with fish, meat or tofu.

**Snack** DETOX JUICE – get used to making this so that it becomes part of your weekly routine.

## Day Nine – Sunday

**Breakfast** DETOX JUICE – it's good to start the day with a cleanse when you have time (can be done in the week too). Have a handful of nuts and seeds as well to provide protein and slow down sugar release from the juiced fruits.

**Lunch** Try having the roast dinner (see last week) at lunchtime so you have more time to burn off calories. You do not have to have meat; a piece of fish or a whole baked trout can be just as satisfying. Keep some aside to make a salad with tomorrow.

**Dinner** TERIYAKI TOFU & VEGETABLE STIR-FRY – light and quick for a relaxing Sunday evening.

**Snack** STRAWBERRY & PEACH SMOOTHIE.

## Day Ten – Monday

**Breakfast** Try things other than milk to go with your cereal, such as bio yogurt, unsweetened soya, oat or rice milk.

**Lunch** Use the extra meat, fish

▼ **That's entertainment**
These healthy meals are perfect for dinner parties.

▲ **Pep up your veg**
Vegetables can be more exciting and varied than you might think.

or chicken you cooked on Sunday to put together a salad. Add some tinned artichokes or sun-dried tomatoes.
**Dinner** SESAME PRAWN NOODLE SALAD.
**Snack** Hard-boiled eggs make great, transportable snacks.

## Day Eleven – Tuesday

**Breakfast** Fresh fruit salad.
**Lunch** ROASTED RED ONION, AVOCADO & SPINACH SALAD – with brown rice or rye bread, if needed.
**Dinner** SEAFOOD SKEWERS WITH ROCKET SALAD.
**Snack** Crudités – slice vegetables such as celery, cucumber, red pepper and carrot.

## Day Twelve – Wednesday

**Breakfast** Choice of any from last week.

**Lunch** FRESH TUNA NIÇOISE.

**Dinner** TURKEY KOFTAS WITH LEMON COUSCOUS
or LASAGNE WITH ROASTED VEGETABLES.

**Snack** Keep reaching for those apples.

## Day Thirteen – Thursday

**Breakfast** Choice of any from last week.

**Lunch** GLAZED SALMON FILLET WITH ASPARAGUS.

**Dinner** BAKED LEMON HADDOCK WITH CHUNKY SALSA
or TERIYAKI TOFU & VEGETABLE STIR-FRY.

**Snack** Choose from the variety of healthy snacks that you should
now be used to having to hand.

## Day Fourteen – Friday

**Breakfast** Think about which is your favourite and most practical
breakfast because you will invariably gravitate towards this more
often. Still try to have variety, though, and a bigger breakfast when
you have time.

**Lunch** Make a salad of your choice with as many of your favourite
salad items as possible so that you really enjoy it.

**Dinner** Treat yourself to a Friday night takeaway –
choosing is the key here. Thai food is light, and
has plenty of spices, garlic and ginger that are
good for weight loss. Avoid anything deep-
fried, but opt instead for a clear soup,
fish, chicken or prawns with vegetables
and a little steamed rice. Splash out –
the better the restaurant, the less oily
and fresher the ingredients will be.

**Snack** Have a little treat to
congratulate yourself on all your hard
work. A small bar of dark, organic
chocolate will provide satisfaction and
also the beneficial properties of cocoa
without the problematic milk solids and too
much sugar. Denying yourself everything can
take the joy out of life, so the occasional weekly
treat is good for you and keeps the willpower up.

▼ **Just reward**
An occasional treat helps to keep
that vital motivation going.

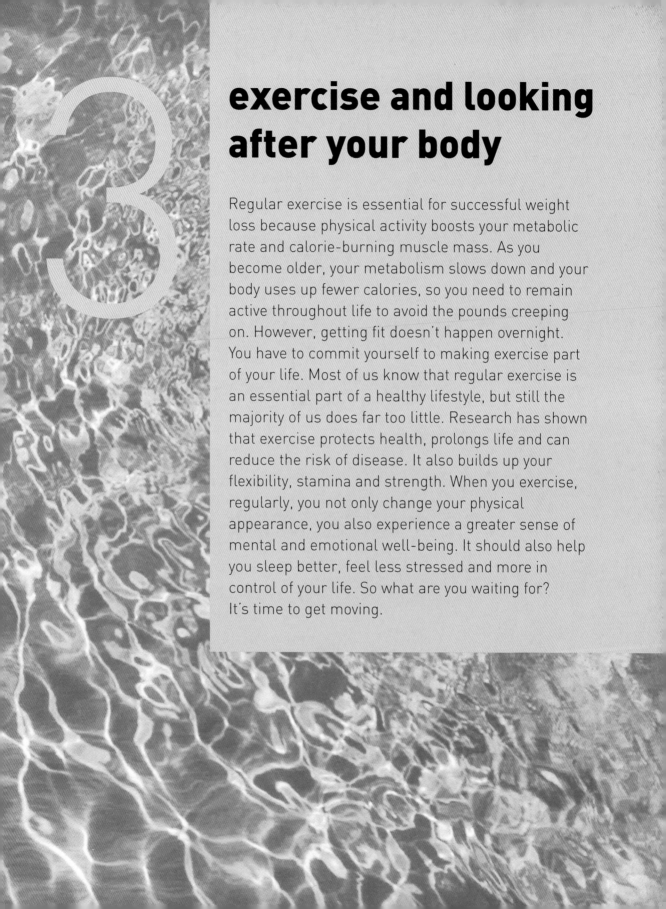

# exercise and looking after your body

Regular exercise is essential for successful weight loss because physical activity boosts your metabolic rate and calorie-burning muscle mass. As you become older, your metabolism slows down and your body uses up fewer calories, so you need to remain active throughout life to avoid the pounds creeping on. However, getting fit doesn't happen overnight. You have to commit yourself to making exercise part of your life. Most of us know that regular exercise is an essential part of a healthy lifestyle, but still the majority of us does far too little. Research has shown that exercise protects health, prolongs life and can reduce the risk of disease. It also builds up your flexibility, stamina and strength. When you exercise, regularly, you not only change your physical appearance, you also experience a greater sense of mental and emotional well-being. It should also help you sleep better, feel less stressed and more in control of your life. So what are you waiting for? It's time to get moving.

# all about exercise

Half the battle with exercise is getting started in the first place and then keeping it up on a regular basis, but there are plenty of good reasons to keep you going. Both your body and your mind benefit from physical activity. When you exercise, your brain releases chemicals called endorphins that make you feel relaxed and in a better mood. Exercise can help with depression, and the feeling of well-being that follows exercise also reduces stress and tension.

The physical benefits of activity are tremendous. If you exercise regularly, your heart muscles become stronger and are able to pump blood more efficiently. As a result, blood pressure is lowered and cholesterol levels reduced as the blood flows more quickly around the body, picking up fatty deposits and waste products, reducing your risk of developing heart disease or having a stroke. The lungs also become stronger and your body more efficient at using oxygen. Joint mobility and stability are improved, which can help to keep you independent and active in later life. Bones stay strong and healthy, and muscles become stronger.

## Different types of exercise

Any type of activity that gives the heart and lungs a good workout is known as aerobic activity. Types of aerobic exercise include swimming, dancing, skating, running, cycling, football, rowing and racket sports. Just as important for fitness are flexibility and strength. Flexibility exercises (stretching) make your joints and muscles more supple; strength exercises such as weightlifting make your muscles stronger, help reduce body fat and make your body appear more toned. Strength and flexibility make you less likely to injure yourself when going about your daily activities or when exercising.

### Getting started

To start exercising, choose an exercise you enjoy, because you are much more likely to do it regularly. Plan when you are going to do it – scheduling exercise helps you to continue. It's great to start exercising when you're on a diet, but if you want to keep the weight off you're going to have to stay active in the long term.

Experts recommend that we should spend half an hour exercising at least five times a week. They all agree that little and often is effective, which may suit you better than a more structured workout. As you become fitter, you can increase the amount of exercise you do and the time you spend doing it. Always be aware of how your body feels during and after exercise. Build up gradually, especially if you have not exercised for a while.

◀ **Look after your body**
Regular exercise will help you lose weight and keep it off.

**Caution**
Consult your doctor if you have not exercised for several years, if you are very overweight, if you are pregnant, if you are over 45 years of age, if you have a history of high blood pressure or high cholesterol, if you have heart or lung disease or any long-standing medical condition. Certain types of exercise may not be appropriate for you.

**DON'T PANIC!**
Exercise tones and builds muscle, which actually weighs more than fat. As you become fitter, your weight may increase slightly. However, muscles burn up more calories than fat, so this weight shouldn't stay on for long if you're watching what you eat. It's important to remember that you are becoming fitter, not fatter. Exercise also increases your appetite so you need to be very careful to resist eating too much.

# how to fit exercise into your day

Most of us complain that we simply don't have the time to exercise regularly, but exercising doesn't have to mean heading off to the gym five times a week for a gruelling workout. The key words are little and often – just 10 minutes once or twice a day can make a significant impact on your fitness levels. Attack the housework with vigour, walk or cycle to work if you can, garden with a vengeance, get intimate with your partner or just dance around the kitchen to your favourite tunes. And try to spend some of your leisure time being active – a long walk after Sunday lunch will benefit all the family.

## Perfect posture

If your posture is good, you'll look thinner and taller. Notice how when you lift your chin up and pull in your stomach muscles you feel trimmer and more confident. The trick is to make this second nature. Not only will you look better, but you will also benefit physically. Good posture keeps the body in its correct position, reduces the strain on your back and allows the internal organs to function efficiently. Poor posture stops you breathing properly, strains muscles and ligaments and over time can push your body out of shape. Joint inflammation, pain and stiffness may also develop.

Good posture looks natural and relaxed, not slouched or hunched. When standing, your neck should be in line with your spine with your head balanced squarely on top, your shoulder blades set back and down and your spine long and naturally curving. Stand with your feet hip-width apart. Gently pull up through your legs, keeping your knees slightly bent. Lengthen your spine, pull in your stomach muscles and stand tall. Keep your shoulders down and relaxed so that your neck is as long as possible. Perfect posture takes practice, but when you've mastered the technique you'll reap the benefits.

▲ **Clean up and shape up**
Vacuum cleaning, ironing – even dusting – will all help to improve your fitness level.

## HOW TO BURN CALORIES WITHOUT EVEN REALIZING IT

Exercise is not just something you do at the gym – it's an integral part of your everyday life. If you'd rather have your teeth pulled than go to an exercise class, take comfort from the fact that exercise doesn't have to be hard or boring. Just look for ways to use energy and you can greatly increase the amount of exercise you take. Start by simply hiding the TV's remote control! Get off the bus one stop further from home, walk up and down escalators, wash your car by hand instead of using the carwash, use a basket rather than a trolley in the supermarket. The possibilities are endless.

## The right equipment and clothing

Proper shoes are key to preventing strains and sprains. Invest in a decent pair of trainers appropriate to your chosen sport – specialist sports shops should be able to advise you. Wear loose, comfortable clothing so that your skin can breathe and so that your movements won't be restricted. If you are exercising outside, wear layers of clothes that can be removed as you warm up.

# take a deep breath

Breathing is something you do automatically, but it can be consciously controlled. It's well known that if you're feeling agitated, taking a deep breath will calm you down. Unfortunately, years of stress and poor lifestyle means shallow, rapid breathing is the norm for most of us, whereby we use only the top third of our lungs. If you don't breathe properly you will restrict your oxygen supply and raise your blood pressure. Correct breathing comes from the deepest area of the lungs and benefits both your body and mind. You'll benefit from a lower heart rate, reduced blood pressure and lower levels of stress hormones. Breathing properly is essential when you're exercising - the rule is to breathe in just before you make a movement and breathe out with each effort.

## The right frame of mind

Positive thinking will motivate you to start an exercise programme, keep you on track and even work out more effectively. A positive mental attitude helps you to succeed because it does not allow thoughts of failure. One way to become more positive is to repeat statements (affirmations) to keep you on track, such as 'I am becoming fit and healthy' or 'Exercise is great and I can feel the benefits already.' Repeat your personal mantras several times a day or write them down and stick them where you will see them – on a mirror or on the fridge door. Soon you will start to believe them.

### HOW TO BREATHE DEEPLY

The following exercise, known as abdominal breathing, will help you breathe more deeply, but it can be quite difficult to master. Here the diaphragm, the sheet of muscle forming the top of the abdomen, is used to help the lungs inflate and deflate without effort. You may feel a little dizzy when you start to do this – it's because you're taking in more oxygen than you're used to.

**1** Sit comfortably. Put one hand on your chest and the other just below the breastbone. Breathe in slowly through your nose.

**2** Hold the breath for a few seconds, then breathe out slowly through your mouth. Expel as much air as you can.

**3** Repeat three or four times. Try to concentrate on your breathing as you do this rather than anything else.

## Mind over matter

Visualization is a technique that uses the imagination to help you fulfil your potential. It is commonly used by athletes in preparation

**▲ The power of nature**
Visualizing a favourite place can help you to achieve a positive frame of mind.

for competition. Motivation can be boosted by mentally rehearsing the sequence of events required for a successful performance. According to the theory, if visualization is repeated enough, expectations rise and you begin to act as if the image were a reality. So you can use visualization to keep up with your exercise programme, envisaging your slimline, toned body, and also as a means of sticking to a sensible eating programme, envisaging the weight dropping off. Anyone can visualize, though it may take a little practice. Just find a quiet place, lie down or sit in a comfortable chair, and close your eyes. Breathe slowly and try to relax before focusing on your chosen mental image.

# basic body workouts

Try to get used to doing some body exercises once a day. The following pages show you exercises to shape up and slim down your body. It's up to you how many you do – as you become fitter, you can build up the amount. Start by doing at least five of each, unless otherwise instructed, and make sure your movements are slow and controlled.

## Warming up and cooling down

Always follow a routine to stretch your muscles, tendons and ligaments before and after exercising. This makes you less likely to injure yourself and helps avoid muscle strain and stiffness. Warming up should involve aerobic exercise such as jogging on the spot for a few minutes followed by a series of stretches. Unless otherwise instructed, repeat the stretches on both sides of your body and try to hold each stretch for at least five seconds.

### ◀ Whole body stretch

**1** Stand tall, arms by your side and feet slightly apart.
**2** Raise your arms straight above your head.
**3** Clasp your hands together. Now stretch your arms up as high as you can. You will feel the stretch in your arms, chest, abdomen, hips and thighs. Repeat three times.

### ▲ Torso-twister

**1** Sit on the floor with one leg straight and the other bent and crossed over it.
**2** Turn towards the bent knee, place the opposite arm in front of the knee and push against that leg while turning your body towards your other arm.

## ▶ Hip and thigh stretch

**1** Kneel with one knee directly above its ankle and stretch the other leg back so that the knee touches the floor.

**2** Place your hands on your front knee to stabilize yourself.

## ▶ Side stretch

**1** Stand up straight with your feet shoulder-width apart.

**2** Put one arm over your head, lean from the waist and reach slowly to the side with your upper hand.

# upper body

Say goodbye to unsightly bat wing arms with these fabulous firming exercises! They'll also sculpt your torso.

## ▼ Hands, arms and shoulders

**1** Stand tall with your feet slightly apart. With your upper arms against your body, bunch your fists at shoulder level.
**2** Stretch up with your right arm, spreading your fingers as wide as possible.

**3** Look up at your hand and stretch for a count of five. Clench your fist again and return to the starting position.
**4** Repeat with your left arm.
**5** Now stretch up with both arms, spreading your fingers wide. Look up at the ceiling and stretch for a count of five. Return with clenched fists to the starting position.

## ▶ Dips

**1** Before starting this exercise, place a chair against a wall.
**2** Stand with your back to the chair, bend your legs and grasp the seat of the chair.
**3** With your bottom raised and your back straight, slowly bend your elbows to about 90 degrees as you lower your bottom towards the floor.
**4** Straighten your arms to return to the starting point.

## ▶ Arms, shoulders and sides

**1** Stand with feet hip-width apart.

**2** Clasp hands above your head, palms upwards and stretch towards the ceiling.

**3** From your waist, bend to the right, keeping your arms stretched.

**4** Return to the centre and bend to your left.

## ▶ Arm and chest muscles

**1** Stand tall with your feet slightly apart, arms straight out to the sides at shoulder level, palms facing upwards.

**2** Make small circles with your arms, increasing to large circles. Return to small circles.

# stomach and waist

Keeping your stomach muscles trim is key to preventing lower back pain and enabling you to perform arm and leg exercises safely and efficiently. We tend to store extra fat around our waists and you'll get a firmer, flatter midriff by working the abdominal muscles correctly and regularly.

▼ **Basic stomach trimmer**

**1** Lie on your back. Pull your knees in towards your chest.
**2** Thrust your legs straight out at an upward angle, hold for a count of ten, then slowly lower your legs to the floor.

▶ **Waist twists**

**1** Stand with your feet hip-width apart and knees slightly bent.
**2** Tighten your abdominal muscles.
**3** Hold your arms out in front of you, bent at an angle as if you were a hula dancer.
**4** Twist your shoulders and head around to one side, then return to the centre, keeping your hips still as you do so. Repeat on the other side of your body.

## ▲ Advanced stomach trimmer

**1** Lie on your back with your feet hip-width apart and your feet firmly on the floor. Keep your knees bent.

**2** Rest your hands on your thighs.

**3** Use your stomach muscles to lift your shoulders gently off the floor, then lower.

**4** Your back should remain in contact with the floor at all times.

**5** To make this exercise even more difficult, cross your hands over your chest.

## ▶ Side bends

**1** Stand with your feet hip-width apart, knees slightly bent.

**2** Tighten your stomach muscles and slide one hand down the side of your leg.

**3** Return to the centre and repeat on the other side.

# lower body exercises

Who wants a sagging bottom or wobbly thighs? Practise these exercises for lissom legs and buttocks of steel!

### ▼ Inner thigh muscles

**1** Lie on your back, legs straight up, feet pointing towards the ceiling.

**2** Bend your knees and imagine you are a frog. Slowly spread your legs out to the sides as far as possible.

**3** Return to the starting position.

### ◀ Hips and thighs

**1** Lie on your back, knees bent, arms out to the sides.

**2** Keeping your knees together, swing them over to the left, until your left leg touches the floor.

**3** Make sure both shoulders stay flat on the floor. Then repeat on your right side. Repeat ten times each side.

### ◀ Legs

**1** Lie on your left side, with your head supported by your left forearm, with your legs together and your right hand on the floor in front of you for support.

**2** Keep your hips facing forward and your body in a straight line.

**3** Bend both knees back. Gently raise the top leg, then lower. Repeat ten times, tensing your buttock as you raise and lower your leg.

**4** Repeat on your right side with your left leg.

### ◀ Buttocks

**1** Sit on the floor, legs straight in front of you and arms folded across your chest.

**2** 'Walk' on your buttocks – ten steps forward, ten steps back.

# facial workout

Muscles have to be exercised to stay firm and fit and this applies to your face just as much as to your body. Facial muscles are different from the rest of the body in that they are directly attached to the skin that covers them. When the facial muscles droop, so does the skin attached to them. Practise the following exercises twice a day to retain your youthful looks and keep your face as toned and fit as your body.

For the sitting exercises, sit in front of a mirror so that you can make sure you are exercising properly. Keep your back teeth together, lips slightly apart, and try not to squint or tense your eye muscles.

### ▶ Cheeks

**1** Grin as widely as you can and hold for a count of five. Repeat twice.
**2** Snarl upwards using the muscles on either side of your nose and hold for a count of five. Repeat twice.
**3** Assume a relaxed smile with your lips closed, then suck your cheeks onto your teeth. Hold for a count of ten. Repeat ten times.

### ◀ Eyes

**1** Press two fingers on either side of your head at the temples while opening and closing your eyes rapidly. Repeat five times.
**2** Sit upright with your eyes closed. While keeping your eyes closed, look up then down as far as possible. Repeat ten times.
**3** Sit upright, looking straight ahead with your eyes open. Look up then down while keeping your head still. Repeat ten times, then look left, then right. Repeat ten times.

## ▷ Neck and chin

**1** Slap lightly under your chin with the back of your hand about 30 times in quick succession.

**2** Sit up straight, tilt your head back and look at the ceiling while keeping your mouth closed. Start to chew slowly. Repeat 20 times.

**3** Jut your chin forwards and very slightly upwards. Place your lower lip over your top lip. Slowly smile up and out. Hold for a count of five, gently stroking upwards with the back of your hand along your jaw line. You should feel a good pull around your jaw line and throat. Gradually release your lip hold and relax. Repeat five times.

## ◁ Forehead

**1** This exercise can be done seated, standing, or lying down facing the ceiling. Lift your eyebrows as high as possible, opening your eyes very wide. Relax and repeat ten times.

**2** Using your fingers, lightly stroke from the bridge of your nose on each side of your face up and out along your forehead to your hairline. Repeat five times.

**3** Place the pads of your fingertips along your hairline. Push upwards gently and hold the skin against the bone. Look straight ahead. Now try to bring your brow down against the resistance of your hold, closing your eyes gradually. Hold this downward pull for a count of three, then slowly relax. Repeat three times.

# skin care

At first glance, information about skin care may not seem to have much place in your programme to lose weight. However, one of the results of not eating properly or exercising is that our bodies become loaded with toxins that may then be converted into an unsightly substance called cellulite. This is an accumulation of fat, fluid and toxins that have become trapped in the deeper layers of your skin, giving it a lumpy, dimpled appearance. Most women, even if they are very slim, have some cellulite because they are genetically programmed to store fat, but excess weight makes it look much worse.

Beauty experts believe that a daily and weekly body care routine, which can easily be carried out at home, will increase the elimination of toxins, helping you to get rid of fat. Specific body treatments, from exfoliation to skin brushing, will leave you feeling pampered and will significantly improve the appearance of your skin and the efficiency of your body's elimination processes.

## Skin brushing

Skin is your body's largest organ, losing about 0.5 kg/1 lb 2 oz of waste products every day through its pores. Skin brushing helps clear the pores and makes your skin glow. It also improves blood and lymph circulation, helping to relieve water retention and enabling the more efficient removal of waste products from the cells.

## How to brush your skin

Use a loofah, a dry flannel, a dry, rough towel or a long-handled, natural bristle brush. Always brush your skin when dry, not wet, and never brush the face as the skin here is very delicate. Follow the sequence below and spend about five minutes a day brushing

▲ **Water power**
A blast of cold water after a hot shower can help to perk up your circulation.

your skin. Strokes should be long and firm and made in the direction of your heart.

**1** Brush both sides of your feet and up your legs.
**2** Brush over your chest and towards the heart. Using gentle, circular strokes, brush your stomach in a clockwise direction.
**3** Raise each arm and brush along from your hand to your armpit.
**4** To finish, brush from your bottom up your back to your neck as far as you can reach.

## Exfoliation

This describes the process of removing dead skin cells. It gives your skin a deep clean, helping it to get rid of impurities, and should be done once a week. Relax in a warm bath for 10 minutes, then rub your body all over with an exfoliating scrub – you can buy one or make your own. Pay particular attention to areas of rough skin and rub as hard as is comfortable. Wash the exfoliant off in the bath, then get out and gently pat yourself dry. Apply a body oil or thick moisturizer to help keep your skin soft and retain moisture.

▲ **Deep clean**
Regular exfoliation will improve your skin's appearance.

## Showering

Every day, a hot shower followed by a blast of cold water will do wonders for your skin and circulation. Alternate 3 minutes of hot water and 1 minute of cold water, at least once, for maximum results.

# recipes

This collection of recipes has been created with taste, variety and health in mind. You are guaranteed not to feel deprived with our cleansing juices, hearty soups, substantial salads, and low-fat meat and fish dishes, not forgetting impressive vegetarian options. Many of the recipes are also low in carbohydrates and gluten-free, and where fats are included, they are usually the healthier ones, such as the omega-3 fatty acids found in oily fish. The emphasis is on fresh produce that provides a wide range of vitamins, minerals and fibre – the ingredients for good health.

# JUICES AND SMOOTHIES
## detox juice

This morning energizer contains beetroot, one of the most effective liver-cleansing vegetables.

2 dessert apples

115 g/4 oz white seedless grapes

1 large carrot

55 g/2 oz cooked beetroot in natural juices

1 cm/½ inch piece of fresh root ginger

**Preparation time** 5 minutes **Serves 1**

1 Quarter the apples, then put them through a juicer along with the grapes, carrot, beetroot and ginger. Serve immediately.

**One serving contains:**
**Energy kCal** 394.25
**Protein g** 3.42
**Carbohydrate g** 99.53
**Sugars g** 78.95 **Fat g** 2.51
**Saturates g** 0.52
**Fibre g** 16.08 (before juicing – most lost in process)
**Sodium g** 0.07

# strawberry and peach smoothie

Try to use natural live bio-yogurt when making this smoothie as it contains beneficial bacteria that are good for the digestive system. If peaches are out of season, you could try bananas instead.

**1 peach**

**140 g/5 oz strawberries**

**250 ml/9 fl oz natural live bio-yogurt**

**Preparation time** 5 minutes **Serves 1**

1 Peel and stone the peach, then roughly chop. Hull the strawberries and halve if large. Put the fruit into a blender with the yogurt and blend until smooth and creamy. Serve immediately.

**One serving contains:**
**Energy kCal** 269.04
**Protein g** 12.53
**Carbohydrate g** 35.6
**Sugars g** 29.94 **Fat g** 7.93
**Saturates g** 1.97
**Fibre g** 3.91
**Sodium g** 1.56

# italian bean and pasta soup

This classic minestrone-style soup is hearty enough to be eaten as a meal in itself.

1½ tbsp olive oil

1 onion, diced

1 celery stick, thinly sliced

1 large carrot, roughly chopped

1 bay leaf

1 tsp dried oregano

1.4 litres/2½ pints vegetable stock

400 g/14 oz tomato passata

175 g/6 oz dried pasta shapes, such as penne or conchiglie

250 g/9 oz canned cannellini beans, drained and rinsed

200 g/7 oz fresh spinach leaves, tough stalks removed

40 g/1½ oz Parmesan cheese shavings (optional)

salt and pepper

**One serving contains:**

**Energy kCal** 349.30

**Protein g** 15.29

**Carbohydrate g** 53.72

**Sugars g** 5.46 **Fat g** 8.97

**Saturates g** 1.66

**Fibre g** 6.97

**Sodium g** 1.12

**Preparation time** 10 minutes

**Cooking time** 30 minutes **Serves 4**

1 Heat the olive oil in a large, heavy-based saucepan. Add the onion and cook, covered, over a medium-low heat for 8 minutes until softened. Add the celery, carrot and bay leaf and cook, stirring occasionally, for a further 3 minutes.

2 Add the oregano, stock and passata and bring to the boil. Reduce the heat, cover, and simmer for 5 minutes.

3 Stir in the pasta and beans, bring back to a rolling boil and cook for about 10 minutes, uncovered, until the pasta is tender but still al dente. Stir occasionally to prevent the pasta sticking.

4 Add the spinach and cook for a further 2 minutes or until the spinach has wilted. Season with salt and pepper to taste and divide the soup between 4 bowls. Sprinkle with the Parmesan just before serving.

# carrot and red lentil soup

This thick, nutritious soup is a good source of vitamins, minerals and fibre. Serve with seeded wholemeal rolls as a light meal.

1½ tbsp olive oil

1 large onion, chopped

1 celery stick, chopped

4 carrots, chopped

200 g/7 oz red lentils, rinsed

2 fresh rosemary sprigs, each about 10 cm/4 inches in length

1 bay leaf

1.4 litres/2½ pints vegetable stock

salt and pepper

**Preparation time** 15 minutes

**Cooking time** 45 minutes **Serves 4**

1 Heat the oil in a large heavy-based saucepan. Add the onion, cover the pan, and cook for 8 minutes over a medium-low heat until softened. Add the celery and carrots, then cook for a further 3 minutes, stirring occasionally.

2 Add the lentils, rosemary, bay leaf and stock, then bring to the boil. Reduce the heat and simmer, half-covered, for 30 minutes or until the lentils are very soft. Occasionally skim off any foam that rises to the surface while cooking the lentils.

3 Remove the rosemary sprigs and bay leaf, then transfer the soup to a blender or use a hand-held blender. Blend the soup until smooth. Return the soup to the pan, season with salt and pepper and reheat if necessary.

**One serving contains:**

**Energy kCal** 264.36

**Protein g** 13.63

**Carbohydrate g** 40.22

**Sugars g** 6.95 **Fat g** 4.04

**Saturates g** 0.23

**Fibre g** 0.16

**Sodium g** 8.13

# thai chicken broth

This light, low-fat soup is packed with flavour. You could serve it with egg or rice noodles for a more substantial light meal.

1.7 litres/3 pints chicken stock

2 stalks of lemon grass, peeled, halved lengthways and crushed with the back of a knife

6 slices of fresh root ginger, plus 4 slices peeled and cut into matchsticks

4 kaffir lime leaves

4 tsp Thai fish sauce

4 skinless, boneless chicken breasts, about 140 g/5 oz each

3 garlic cloves, thinly sliced

100 g/3½ oz fresh spinach leaves, tough stalks removed

3 tbsp rice vinegar

2 tbsp lime juice

2 bird's eye chillies, deseeded and finely chopped

salt and pepper

2 tbsp chopped fresh coriander

**Preparation time** 15 minutes
**Cooking time** 25 minutes **Serves 4**

1 Put the chicken stock, lemon grass, 6 ginger slices, lime leaves and fish sauce into a large saucepan. Add the chicken breasts and bring to the boil. Reduce the heat and simmer, half-covered, for 20 minutes.

2 Remove the chicken and set aside, then strain the stock, discarding the solids.

3 Return the stock to the pan and add the ginger matchsticks, garlic, spinach, rice vinegar, lime juice and chillies and simmer for 2–3 minutes.

4 Slice the chicken into strips and divide between 4 bowls. Pour over the soup. Season with salt and pepper, if necessary, and garnish each serving with fresh coriander.

**One serving contains:**
**Energy kCal** 186.33
**Protein g** 34.06
**Carbohydrate g** 5.28
**Sugars g** 1.82 **Fat g** 1.98
**Saturates g** 0.49
**Fibre g** 0.98
**Sodium g** 0.34

# tabbouleh

You could use couscous instead of bulgar wheat to make this refreshing, filling salad. To transform it into a light meal, top with slices of griddled halloumi cheese. Tabbouleh is best served at room temperature.

175 g/6 oz bulgar wheat

450ml/16 fl oz boiling water

8 vine-ripened tomatoes, deseeded and chopped

7.5 cm/3 inch piece of cucumber, diced

3 spring onions, finely chopped

4 tbsp chopped fresh mint

4 tbsp chopped fresh coriander

4 tbsp chopped fresh parsley

8 slices of Greek halloumi cheese (optional)

DRESSING

juice of ½ lemon

2 tbsp extra virgin olive oil

salt and pepper

**Preparation time** 15 minutes

**Cooking time** 3 minutes, plus 25 minutes soaking **Serves 4**

1 Cover the bulgar wheat with the boiling water in a large bowl. Stir and leave for about 20–25 minutes or until the bulgar is tender but still retains some bite. Drain well.

2 Transfer to a serving bowl and leave to cool slightly. Add the tomatoes, cucumber and spring onions and toss until combined. Stir in the herbs.

3 Mix together the lemon juice and olive oil to make the dressing and pour it over the salad. Mix well with a spoon, then season with salt and pepper to taste.

4 If serving with the halloumi, heat a griddle until hot. Place the halloumi on the griddle and cook for about 2–3 minutes, turning halfway. Serve the halloumi on top of the tabbouleh.

**One serving contains:**

**Energy kCal** 336.09

**Protein g** 9.01

**Carbohydrate g** 59.09

**Sugars g** 11.39 **Fat g** 8.91

**Saturates g** 1.19

**Fibre g** 12.5

**Sodium g** 0.04

# griddled venison with orange salsa

Venison is low in fat compared with other types of red meat. Here, it is served with a flavourful orange salsa. You could also accompany it with boiled new potatoes and a mixed green salad.

**ORANGE SALSA**

2 oranges, peeled, segmented and diced

2 shallots, diced

juice and finely grated rind of 2 limes

1–2 hot chillies, finely chopped

2 tbsp extra virgin olive oil

6 tbsp chopped fresh mint

salt and pepper

olive oil, for brushing

4 venison steaks, about 125 g/ 4½ oz each

salt and pepper

**One serving contains:**

**Energy kCal** 356.86

**Protein g** 40.13

**Carbohydrate g** 11.66

**Sugars g** 7.78 **Fat g** 16.63

**Saturates g** 3.34

**Fibre g** 2.10

**Sodium g** 0.07

**Preparation time** 10 minutes

**Cooking time** 10 minutes **Serves 4**

1 To make the salsa, put the orange, shallots, lime juice and rind, chilli, olive oil and mint in a bowl. Season to taste with salt and pepper and mix well. Set aside to allow the flavours to merge.

2 Brush a griddle pan with oil and heat until smoking. Season the venison and griddle for 4–5 minutes on each side.

3 Serve each venison steak with 2 large spoonfuls of salsa.

# pasta with italian meatballs

These meatballs are cooked in a rich tomato sauce to keep them moist and succulent, and to avoid having to use extra oil. Serve with a green salad.

400 g/14 oz lean minced pork

1 onion, grated

2 tsp dried oregano

2 garlic cloves, crushed

1 small egg, beaten

salt and pepper

300 g/10½ oz dried wholemeal spaghetti

fresh basil leaves, to garnish (optional)

TOMATO SAUCE

1 tbsp olive oil

2 garlic cloves, chopped

250 ml/9 fl oz dry white wine

600 ml/1 pint tomato passata

1 bay leaf

2 tsp sun-dried tomato purée

**Preparation time** 20 minutes, plus 30 minutes chilling

**Cooking time** 30 minutes **Serves 4**

**One serving contains:**
**Energy kCal** 662.14
**Protein g** 31.74
**Carbohydrate g** 69.06
**Sugars g** 7.25 **Fat g** 26.80
**Saturates g** 8.36
**Fibre g** 2.75
**Sodium g** 0.72

1 Put the minced pork, onion, oregano, garlic and egg in a bowl and mix well until combined. Season with salt and pepper, cover the bowl with clingfilm and refrigerate for 30 minutes.

2 Meanwhile, make the tomato sauce by heating the olive oil in a large sauté pan and frying the garlic over a low heat for 1 minute. Increase the heat, pour in the white wine and boil until the wine has reduced and the smell of alcohol has disappeared. Reduce the heat to medium-low, add the passata, bay leaf and tomato purée, stir well and cook, half-covered, for 5 minutes.

3 Remove the meatball mixture from the refrigerator and form it into walnut-sized balls. Place the meatballs in the tomato sauce and cook, half-covered, over a medium-low heat for 15–20 minutes until they are cooked through.

4 Meanwhile, cook the pasta in boiling salted water following the packet instructions until al dente. Divide between 4 shallow bowls and top with the meatball sauce, garnished with basil.

# turkey koftas with lemon couscous

Lamb is more often used to make koftas but turkey is lower in fat and makes the perfect foil for the aromatic herbs and spices.

500 g/1 lb 2oz minced turkey

1 large onion, finely chopped

2 tbsp chopped fresh coriander

2 tbsp chopped fresh parsley

1 tsp ground coriander

½ tsp chilli powder

1–2 tbsp olive oil

salt and pepper

LEMON COUSCOUS

280 g/10 oz couscous

1 tsp bouillon powder

4 tbsp lemon juice

4 tbsp chopped fresh coriander, plus extra to garnish

salt and pepper

**One serving contains:**
**Energy kCal** 517.36
**Protein g** 31.65
**Carbohydrate g** 59.51
**Sugars g** 4.19 **Fat g** 16.47
**Saturates g** 2.92
**Fibre g** 4.58
**Sodium g** 0.38

**Preparation time** 25 minutes
**Cooking time** 30 minutes **Serves 4**

1 Place the turkey, onion, herbs, ground coriander, chilli powder and salt and pepper seasoning in a food processor, then blend.

2 Divide the mixture into 12 portions and, using wet hands, shape each one around a skewer (soak wooden skewers in water first for 15 minutes, to prevent burning). Refrigerate for 30 minutes.

3 Heat a griddle or frying pan and add half the oil. Cook the skewers in 2 or 3 batches, adding oil if necessary and turning occasionally, for 10 minutes or until browned and cooked through.

4 Meanwhile, make the lemon couscous. Put the couscous in a bowl and pour in enough boiling water to cover by 1cm/½ in. Stir in the bouillon powder. Leave for about 5 minutes until the water has been absorbed, then fluff up with a fork. Stir in the lemon juice and fresh coriander. Season with salt and pepper.

5 Serve 3 skewers per person and accompany with the lemon couscous. Garnish with extra coriander, if liked.

# oriental fish parcels

Cooking the fish in a parcel helps it to retain its moisture and absorb the flavours of the accompanying ingredients. It also helps to seal in nutrients.

4 thick cod fillets, each about 200 g/7 oz

1 garlic clove, thinly sliced

4 thin slices of fresh root ginger, peeled and cut into matchsticks

4 baby leeks, cut into thin strips

2 small carrots, cut into thin strips

½ red pepper, seeded and cut into thin strips

4 tbsp lime juice

4 tsp light soy sauce

2 tbsp fresh apple juice

1 tsp sesame oil

salt and black pepper

fresh coriander, to garnish

**Preparation time** 15 minutes

**Cooking time** 20 minutes **Serves 4**

1 Preheat the oven to 200°C/400°F/Gas Mark 6. Place each cod fillet on a piece of foil or baking paper that is large enough to make a parcel. Arrange some garlic, ginger, leeks, carrots and pepper on top of the pieces of fish.

2 Mix together the lime juice, soy sauce, apple juice and sesame oil, then spoon the mixture over the fish. Season with salt and pepper to taste, then fold the foil or paper to make a loose parcel.

3 Put the parcels on a baking tray and bake for 15–20 minutes, depending on the thickness of the fillets, until the fish is cooked. Carefully open each parcel and transfer the fish and its toppings to 4 plates. Garnish with coriander before serving.

**One serving contains:**

**Energy kCal** 231.65

**Protein g** 37.38

**Carbohydrate g** 13.39

**Sugars g** 5.92 **Fat g** 2.77

**Saturates g** 0.30

**Fibre g** 1.98

**Sodium g** 0.31

# baked lemon haddock with chunky salsa

The tomato and herb salsa adds plenty of oomph to the simply cooked plain fish. Serve with steamed courgettes and broccoli.

4 thick haddock or cod fillets, about 200 g/7 oz each

olive oil, for brushing

8 thin slices of lemon

salt and pepper

SALSA

8 vine-ripened tomatoes, deseeded and diced

2 shallots, diced

2 tbsp olive oil

1 garlic clove, crushed

3 tbsp chopped fresh parsley

3 tbsp chopped fresh basil

juice of 1 lemon

**One serving contains:**
**Energy kCal** 231.65
**Protein g** 37.38
**Carbohydrate g** 13.39
**Sugars g** 5.92 **Fat g** 2.77
**Saturates g** 0.30
**Fibre g** 1.98
**Sodium g** 0.31

**Preparation time** 15 minutes
**Cooking time** 20 minutes **Serves 4**

1 Preheat the oven to 200°C/400°F/Gas Mark 6. Rinse and dry each haddock fillet and place on a piece of foil that is large enough to cover the fish and make a parcel.

2 Brush each fillet with a little olive oil and top with two slices of lemon, then season with salt and pepper. Fold over the foil to encase the fish. Put the parcels in a roasting tin and bake for 15–20 minutes or until just cooked and opaque.

3 Meanwhile, to make the salsa, put the tomatoes, shallots, olive oil, garlic, parsley, basil and lemon juice in a bowl. Mix until combined and season to taste with salt and pepper.

4 Carefully unfold each parcel and arrange the fish and its juices on 4 serving plates. Place a large spoonful of salsa by the side.

# glazed salmon fillet with asparagus

The marinade adds a rich golden glaze to the salmon. You could steam the asparagus instead of griddling it, if preferred.

**MARINADE**

2 garlic cloves, crushed

1 tsp grated fresh root ginger

4 tbsp fresh apple juice

2 tsp maple syrup

2 tbsp soy sauce

1 tsp sunflower oil

salt and pepper

4 salmon fillets, about 140 g/4½ oz each

olive oil, for brushing

20 asparagus spears, trimmed

1 tbsp sesame seeds, lightly toasted

**Preparation time** 15 minutes, plus 1 hour marinating

**Cooking time** 10 minutes **Serves 4**

1 Mix together all the ingredients for the marinade and season with salt and pepper. Place the salmon in a shallow dish and pour the marinade over, turning the fish to ensure it is coated. Cover with clingfilm and marinate in the refrigerator for at least 1 hour, turning the fish occasionally.

2 Preheat the grill to high. Line the grill pan with foil and place the salmon on top. Spoon half of the marinade over the fish and grill for about 6 minutes, turning once, until just cooked but still pink in the centre.

3 Meanwhile, heat a griddle pan and brush it with some olive oil. Arrange the asparagus in the pan and cook for 3–4 minutes until just tender.

4 Place the remaining marinade in a small saucepan and boil. Arrange the asparagus on 4 plates, then top each one with the salmon. Spoon the marinade over the fish and sprinkle with the sesame seeds. Serve immediately.

**One serving contains:**

**Energy kCal** 320.77

**Protein g** 31.13

**Carbohydrate g** 8.76

**Sugars g** 5.69 **Fat g** 17.56

**Saturates g** 3.38

**Fibre g** 2.07

**Sodium g** 0.54

# seafood skewers with rocket salad

These simple sweet chilli marinated kebabs can be barbecued instead of grilled, if preferred. They are served with a lightly dressed rocket salad.

4 tbsp sweet chilli sauce

2 tbsp hot water

2 garlic cloves, crushed

2.5 cm/1 inch piece of fresh root ginger, peeled and grated

½ tsp crushed dried chillies

juice and rind of 2 limes

16 raw tiger prawns, peeled and deveined

225 g/8 oz salmon, skinned and cut into large bite-sized pieces

350 g/12 oz firm white fish, skinned and cut into large bite-sized pieces

salt and pepper

lime wedges, to serve

ROCKET SALAD

100 g/3½ oz rocket leaves

1 tbsp olive oil

1 tsp lemon juice

salt

**Preparation time** 15 minutes, plus 30 minutes marinating
**Cooking time** 5 minutes **Serves 4**

**One serving contains:**
**Energy kCal** 268.12
**Protein g** 33.42
**Carbohydrate g** 8.73
**Sugars g** 4.74 **Fat g** 10.71
**Saturates g** 1.46
**Fibre g** 0.60
**Sodium g** 0.63

1 Mix together the sweet chilli sauce, hot water, garlic, ginger, chillies and lime juice and rind in a shallow dish. Add the prawns, salmon and white fish to the dish and turn to coat them in the marinade. Season with salt and pepper to taste. Cover the dish with clingfilm and marinate for 30 minutes in the refrigerator.

2 Preheat the grill to high and line the pan with foil. Divide the fish and prawns between 8 skewers, starting and finishing each one with a prawn.

3 Arrange the skewers in the grill pan and spoon over half the marinade. Grill for 2 minutes, turn and spoon over the rest of the marinade and grill for a further 2–3 minutes. Place 2 skewers on each plate and pour over any marinade left in the grill pan.

4 To make the rocket salad, toss the rocket leaves in the olive oil and lemon juice and season with salt. Serve with the skewers and lime wedges.

# mushroom, bean and spinach tower

This impressive looking dish makes a perfect dinner party main course served with new potatoes and a salad.

2 tbsp olive oil, plus extra for brushing

8 large portobello mushrooms

4 tbsp water

1 courgette, sliced lengthways into 4, then halved

350 g/12 oz fresh spinach leaves, tough stalks removed

2 large garlic cloves, crushed

225 g/8 oz canned cannellini beans, drained and rinsed

2 tsp dried oregano

4 tbsp half-fat crème fraîche

salt and pepper

**One serving contains:**
**Energy kCal** 277.31
**Protein g** 16.84
**Carbohydrate g** 38.51
**Sugars g** 11.01 **Fat g** 9.26
**Saturates g** 1.64
**Fibre g** 11.23
**Sodium g** 0.44

**Preparation time** 20 minutes

**Cooking time** 25 minutes **Serves 4**

1 Preheat the oven to 200°C/400°F/Gas Mark 6. Place 4 pieces of foil on a work surface and brush with oil. Place 2 mushrooms on top of one another on each piece. Brush the mushroom tops with oil, season with salt and pepper and add 1 tablespoon of water. Fold the foil to make a parcel.

2 Place the parcels on a baking tray and bake for 20–25 minutes until the mushrooms are tender.

3 Meanwhile, steam the courgette and spinach for 2–3 minutes until tender. Keep warm. Heat the oil in a heavy-based saucepan and add the garlic, beans and oregano. Cook over medium-low heat for 2 minutes. Add the crème fraîche and heat through. Put the mixture in a blender and purée until smooth. Season with salt and pepper.

4 To serve, place a mushroom on each plate, top with a slice of courgette, a spoonful of spinach and the bean purée. Add the remaining courgette and spinach, and top with a mushroom.

# lasagne with roasted vegetables

This lasagne dispenses with the rich, high calorie béchamel and meat sauces.

2 tbsp extra virgin olive oil

1 tbsp balsamic vinegar

2 fresh rosemary sprigs

2 red peppers, deseeded and quartered

2 courgettes, sliced lengthways

2 red onions, peeled and each cut into 8 wedges

1 fennel bulb, sliced into thin wedges

8 vine-ripened tomatoes

1 head of garlic, unpeeled and top sliced off

16 black olives

8 sheets of dried lasagne

salt and pepper

shavings of fresh Parmesan cheese, to serve (optional)

## PESTO DRESSING

1½ tbsp good quality pesto

1 tbsp olive oil

1 tbsp hot water

**One serving contains:**
**Energy kCal** 359.11
**Protein g** 8.44
**Carbohydrate g** 45.23
**Sugars g** 13.61 **Fat g** 18.29
**Saturates g** 1.65
**Fibre g** 7.85
**Sodium g** 0.32

**Preparation time** 20 minutes, plus 1 hour marinating
**Cooking time** 40 minutes **Serves 4**

1 Mix together the olive oil, vinegar and rosemary in a large shallow dish. Place the red pepper, courgette, red onion, fennel, tomatoes and garlic in the dish and toss them in this mixture. Leave to marinate for at least 1 hour.

2 Preheat the oven to 200°C/400°F/Gas Mark 6. Put all the vegetables except the tomatoes in a roasting tin with the marinade. Roast for 25 minutes, then remove the rosemary and garlic. Add the tomatoes and olives, then return to the oven and cook for another 15 minutes or until the vegetables are tender.

3 Meanwhile, squeeze out the soft roasted garlic from each clove, mash with a fork and set aside. Mix together the ingredients for the pesto dressing. Cook the sheets of lasagne in plenty of salted boiling water following the packet instructions, then drain.

4 To serve, place a sheet of lasagne on each plate and top with the roasted vegetables and garlic purée. Place another sheet of lasagne on top and add the pesto dressing and Parmesan, if liked.

# teriyaki tofu and vegetable stir-fry

Tofu is a nutritious, low-fat ingredient made from soya beans. Its mild flavour means that it is best marinated before cooking.

3 tbsp teriyaki sauce

1 tbsp hot water

250 g/9 oz tofu, dried in kitchen towel and cut into cubes

1 tbsp groundnut or vegetable oil

splash of toasted sesame oil

350 g/12 oz broccoli florets

175 g/6 oz fine green beans, trimmed

3 spring onions, sliced on the diagonal

4 pak choi, sliced in half

2 garlic cloves, chopped

2.5 cm/1 inch piece of fresh root ginger, peeled and finely chopped

6 tbsp fresh apple juice

4 tsp soy sauce

fresh coriander leaves, to garnish

**Preparation time** 15 minutes, plus 1 hour marinating

**Cooking time** 20 minutes **Serves 4**

1 Put the teriyaki sauce and water in a shallow dish. Add the tofu and carefully turn it in the sauce until completely coated. Cover with clingfilm and marinate in the refrigerator for at least 1 hour.

2 Preheat the oven to 200°C/400°F/Gas Mark 6. Put the tofu and marinade in a roasting tin and cook for 20 minutes, turning occasionally, until slightly crisp and golden on the outside.

3 Meanwhile, heat a frying pan or wok and add both the groundnut and sesame oils. Add the broccoli and green beans, then stir-fry, tossing the vegetables continuously, for 5 minutes.

4 Add the spring onions, pak choi, garlic and ginger and stir-fry for another 1 minute. Pour in the apple juice and soy sauce and cook for 1–2 minutes, adding a little extra water if the stir-fry appears dry.

5 Divide the stir-fry between 4 shallow bowls and top with the tofu. Garnish with coriander just before serving.

**One serving contains:**
**Energy kCal** 333.37
**Protein g** 29.21
**Carbohydrate g** 36.36
**Sugars g** 13.71 **Fat g** 13.48
**Saturates g** 1.80
**Fibre g** 13.99
**Sodium g** 1.70

# 5 beyond dieting

For most people, the hardest part of weight control is not losing weight but keeping it off. However, it is possible, as long as you believe that you can control your weight, and combine sensible eating habits with a regular exercise regime. If you go back to your old habits you'll just put the weight back on and continue to gain. This is the main problem with crash diets – they don't help you make lifestyle changes that you can keep up in the long term.

Successful slimmers are those who've not only lost weight but managed to keep it off for good. They support themselves by self-monitoring to stay conscious of their habits, whether it's through ongoing calorie awareness or keeping an occasional food diary. In this section, you'll find strategies to help you cope with those scenarios that throw you into nutritional chaos. Stay positive, congratulate yourself on what you've achieved so far and believe in yourself. You can control your weight for life.

# damage limitation

Just when you feel you're looking great, completely in control of your eating habits and have bags of energy to spare, life hits you with a crisis or obstacle, and all your good intentions disappear along with a large tub of ice cream. Then you start to feel annoyed with yourself, can't be bothered to exercise and, even worse, feel that you've let yourself down. Don't despair, read through the following pages to identify which scenarios you're vulnerable to and learn how to deal with those diet saboteurs. Forewarned is forearmed!

## Planning

Planning is essential if you want to maintain your svelte shape. Write down possible barriers to achieving your goal and strategies to overcome these. Plan your weekly meals, stock your fridge and larder with healthy snacks and cook ahead if you can so you've always got something healthy and nutritious in the freezer. Planning also involves scheduling exercise (this will make you much more likely to do it), booking time for yourself (a great way to deal with stress) and being aware of when you're entertaining or eating out so that you can adopt the appropriate strategies.

## Food and activity diary

This is one of the biggest guns in your arsenal to deploy in the war against excess weight. Keep a food and activity diary for a week or so before you even embark on your weight loss programme to observe your habits and identify problem areas (see pages 110–111 for an example). Many of us reach for the biscuit tin when we're bored. Anticipate this by writing down the times of the day (or week or month) when you're vulnerable to uncontrolled grazing, then plan a list of activities to do to stop yourself. Keep up the diary during your diet and beyond to keep track of what you're eating – people who do, keep the weight off.

▲ **Write it down**
Monitor your eating and activity habits by keeping a diary.

▶ **Shop sensibly**
Make a list of healthy food in advance – and stick to it!

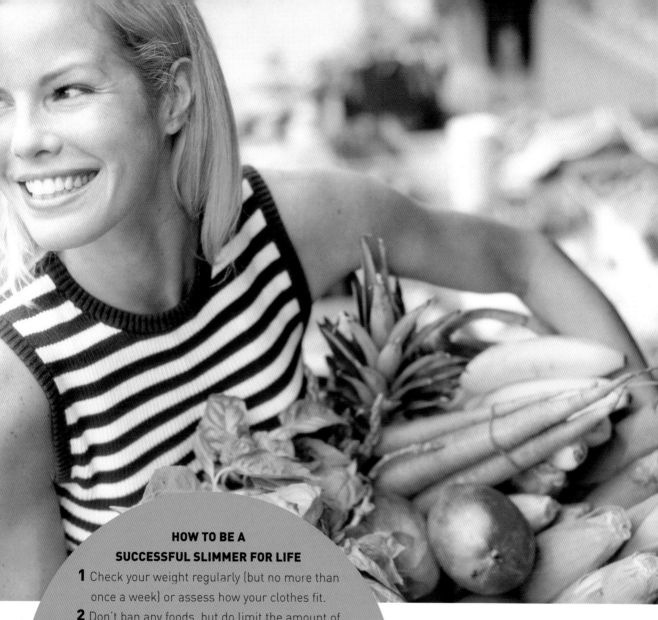

### HOW TO BE A
### SUCCESSFUL SLIMMER FOR LIFE

**1** Check your weight regularly (but no more than once a week) or assess how your clothes fit.

**2** Don't ban any foods, but do limit the amount of those you know will pile on the pounds. This won't do the rest of your family any harm either.

**3** Don't tell yourself off if you overeat.

**4** Address and confront problems rather than trying to eat, drink, smoke, sleep or just wish them away.

**5** Continue to eat a balanced diet with plenty of fruit and vegetables.

**6** Eat regular meals at regular times.

**7** Sit down to eat your meals, take time over them and pay attention to what you're eating.

## Shopping

Never go shopping when you're hungry – you'll end up with a trolley of junk food and nothing nutritious to eat. Always make a list and stick to it. Even better, shop online. You don't have to face the temptation of the biscuit aisle and the money you spend on delivery charges will be cancelled out by the impulse buys you didn't make.

# coping with cravings

By learning to cope with cravings you can stay firmly on track for weight control. Hunger is only one of the reasons why we eat – stress, boredom, a social occasion, loneliness, the smell of food or pure habit are all triggers. Triggers become so automatic that sometimes it really does seem that you can't control what you eat. For those who struggle with their weight, eating when you aren't really hungry is one of the biggest problems.

## Taking charge

Cravings are a perfectly normal response to life and its demands and the good news is that you can control them. How we think affects how we respond to cravings. For example, on a bad morning you may crave a hamburger for lunch, but you still have time to decide whether to give in to the craving or not. Even after buying the food, you can still decide not to eat it. When deliberating, try this: think about the consequences if you eat it, how will you feel physically and how will you feel about yourself? Fat? Slightly sick? Angry? If you don't eat it, how will you feel? Virtuous? In control? Thinner? Now think hard about how you would prefer to feel. Making a conscious decision like this helps you to feel in control of what you eat and to overcome those cravings.

### TOP TIPS FOR DEALING WITH CRAVINGS

**1** Never forbid a food – you'll only want it more.

**2** Don't leave trigger foods in sight or easy reach.

**3** Make yourself a star chart. Every time you resist a craving, award yourself a gold star. When you've got ten, buy yourself a small treat (not food-related!)

**4** Most cravings will go away after about 20 minutes, so try to outlast them. Lock yourself in the bathroom and have a long soak, or go for a walk.

▲ **Treat yourself**
Avoid cravings by taking a long, relaxing bath.

# eating out

Long-term weight management doesn't mean you can't ever go out and have a good time, so here are some creative ideas to help you keep control of what's on your plate.

### Anticipate

If you know you've got an event coming up, try eating a little less the day before. If you can, plan what you are going to eat before you go out so that you're not tempted to over order.

### Don't clear your plate

You don't have to eat everything that's put in front of you, particularly if you are in a restaurant. Your mother is not there to scold you for not clearing the plate (or if she is, remember it's your business, not hers, as to what you eat!).

### Two not three

How many times have you ploughed through the starter, main course and dessert only to find yourself feeling uncomfortably full? Skip the starter or dessert, and avoid the bread basket. You'll save money, too.

### Buffet management

Buffet meals can spell disaster. The trick is to load your plate with the low-calorie options – the vegetables and salads – before finding room for the hunks of bread and the food smothered in mayonnaise. Practise portion control, and eat the low-calorie foods first.

▼ **Choose light**
Order a light meal when you go out to a restaurant to eat.

# new partner

Too many romantic meals washed down with a bottle of wine will play havoc with your waistline. The solution is to keep your romantic meals to a weekly treat, and not be tempted to eat the same amount as your partner – he or she can fill up on extra rice, vegetables or potatoes if they wish. Everyone's metabolism is different, and it's also a sad fact of life that men need more calories than women, which is why men can get away with eating what seems to be twice as much as women without putting on an ounce.

## alcohol

Alcohol is fine in moderation but there are two main reasons why it can sabotage weight control. Firstly, it's an appetite stimulant and secondly, it relaxes your inhibitions so you're more likely to be careless over what you eat. Never drink on an empty stomach – if you know you're going out drinking, eat something light before you go and position yourself well way from the nuts and crisps lined up on the bar (they've probably been coughed over or dipped into by someone whose hands aren't as clean as yours anyway!). Alcohol is full of empty calories and the more you have, the more you want. You're better off limiting your intake to a couple of glasses two or three times a week and you'll appreciate it more, rather than drinking out of habit. Always start an evening out with a soft drink or glass of water and match every alcoholic drink with a non-alcoholic one. That way you're more likely not to binge, and you'll prevent the worst effects of a hangover by staying hydrated.

**BACK ON TRACK**

How to get your eating back under control when you've overdone it.

**1** Phone a friend, family member, contact a slimming club or log on to an online chatroom – whatever suits you. Finding support quickly is essential. Talk about the feelings that may be causing you to overeat. Be honest about what you're eating and actively plan to get yourself motivated again.

**2** Get moving. Don't punish yourself with a 3-hour stint at the gym, but go for a long walk This will work out your mind and body and help relax you.

**3** Write it down. Look at your food diary, write down positive statements and repeat them to yourself. Take responsibility for getting back on track. Look to the long term, think where you want to be this time next year and don't let anything stand in your way.

**4** Stay positive and don't get discouraged by weight gain. It doesn't mean you've blown your weight loss strategy for good. Accept the setbacks and start again now.

**5** Don't deprive yourself. Focus instead on what you're going to eat rather than what you're not going to eat.

◀ **Dinner for two**
Make healthy food a regular part of your romantic meals.

# starting a new job

Whether you're racking up the hours in an attempt to impress or just getting to grips with the workload/commute, this is a prime time for takeaways, missed meals and frequent blasts of caffeine washed down with full-fat milk. One solution is to cook in bulk on your day off so that you've got a stocked freezer and can pop something nutritious in the microwave when you come home. Keep a bowl of fruit on your desk at work to give you vital bursts of energy when you need it, and always have a bottle of water on hand. A glass of water is a far better way to combat a mid-afternoon energy slump than another cup of coffee.

## Living on your own

It's all too easy to fall into a routine of living off microwaveable meals for one when you're single. It doesn't have to be this way, however. With a little planning, you can eat well every day of the week and keep your weight under control.

**1** Write down a meal planner for the next two weeks, and ensure you have a balanced diet. Refer to the meal programme on page 28 for inspiration.

**2** Buy your fruit and vegetables loose. This way, you can buy the amounts you anticipate you'll consume and you won't end up with bags of rotting salad lurking at the bottom of the fridge.

**3** Avoid the supermarket specials and the 'buy one get one free' offers. Buying in bulk usually results in eating in bulk. However, it does make economic sense to buy multipacks of meat or fish and then bag up individual portions to store in the freezer.

**4** Eating alone shouldn't be a joyless affair. Sit down at the table and take time to enjoy your food. You can even light candles and play some background music to enhance the experience.

▼ **Satisfying snacks**
Keep a bowl of fruit to hand to stave off energy slumps.

# having young children

Who can resist the lure of a lukewarm fish finger lingering in a pool of ketchup? You'd never dream of ordering it in a restaurant, but when it's left on junior's plate... The key solution here is to remember that you are not a dustbin! It's a hard habit to break, but don't eat the leftovers. Clear the plates straight away and put the leftovers in the bin. Having children in the house often means a ready supply of crisps, biscuits and cakes, especially if they take packed lunches to school. Keep these products out of your sight and set a good example by snacking on fruit.

## WHAT TO DO WHEN YOU HIT A WEIGHT PLATEAU

**1** Try a new exercise routine. Variety is the spice of life.

**2** Try some new recipes.

**3** Pamper yourself and schedule in some treats (make them non-food ones).

**4** De-junk your wardrobe. Throw out anything shapeless, baggy and dowdy – anything that reminds you of the shape you don't want to be.

**5** Go shopping and buy some sexy new underwear.

**6** Recognize your achievements – tell your friends how much weight you've lost and accept their compliments.

## Tied to the kitchen

This is another hazard of having young children. On the whole, young children tend to eat when they're hungry, which means little and often. It's fine for them, but can be disastrous for you. Even if you've got your children trained to the point that they'll happily tuck into a bowl of hummus and carrot sticks, you'll find yourself salivating and before you know it, you're joining in and eating most of what's on the table, regardless of whether you're hungry or not. Here's how to limit the damage:

**1** If you can't stop yourself from joining in, cut up an apple into small pieces, put it on a plate and sit down and eat with the children.

**2** Make it a rule never to eat standing up and always to eat off a plate. You'll be surprised how much grazing this will stop.

**3** Tape a list of your weight maintenance goals to the fridge door.

**4** Think beyond baking. Remember that you are a role model for your children and that it's good for them to help you make things other than biscuits. Little ones can help you stir up fruit smoothies just as well as cakes.

# time of the month

Many women find that no matter how hard they try, it's almost impossible to control food cravings when they're premenstrual, and this is when bingeing becomes a real temptation. Take comfort from the fact that your metabolic rate increases by about 140 calories a day in the two weeks leading up to your period, so you do actually need to eat a bit more, but not necessarily more chocolate! Try the following solutions:

**1** When you feel food cravings beginning to take hold, reach for low-calorie snacks such as sticks of celery, vegetables or pieces of fruit.

**2** Keep a stock of such healthy snacks to hand – small pots of yogurt, mini boxes of raisins, rice cakes and small bananas, for example.

**3** Some people swear by sniffing vanilla essence – and since satiety is linked to smell, it's certainly worth a try.

**4** Brush your teeth after every meal – this can stop eating between meals in its tracks.

## Let down by weekends

You find it easy to stay in control all week, but somehow when Friday night comes, it's hard to be so stringent. The solution lies in planning ahead – if you know the weekend's going to be non-stop party action, eat 300 calories less the day before and plan to fit in some exercise over the weekend, even if it's just a long walk on Sunday. You could also try eating two meals instead of three on Saturday and Sunday. At the weekends, breakfast often segues into lunchtime, so why not have a healthy mid-morning brunch and skip lunch altogether?

### BREAKFAST: A SIMPLE WAY TO CONTROL YOUR FOOD INTAKE

Eating breakfast can help reduce snacking and avoid overeating later. Scientific evidence shows that the majority of breakfast eaters weigh less than those who skip breakfast. The most satisfying breakfasts work in two ways. They rapidly raise blood sugar levels for a quick burst of energy, which is followed by a longer term energy boost from complex carbohydrate, protein-containing foods that are more slowly digested. If you feel you've no time at home, make yourself a packed breakfast to eat on the train or at your desk – put in a muesli bar, a handful of nuts or a hard-boiled egg (make a batch one evening) and some fresh fruit. You don't have to eat breakfast at the crack of dawn – as long as you eat within several hours of waking up you'll be fine. If you've been skipping breakfast, try a few grapes or a plain oatcake. After a few days your body may feel like something more substantial.

▲ **Soothe your mood**

Fruit will sustain your energy levels and
balance out mood swings by avoiding
stressful sugar surges.

### MORE WAYS TO KEEP MOVING

Keeping the weight off isn't just about
watching what you eat, it's also about keeping
active. Try these easy options to get you moving:

### DIY ACTIVITIES

Decorating will give you a decent activity boost and help you
tick things off your to-do list as well.

### PLAY WITH YOUR CHILDREN

Young children never seem to sit still, so go and play with them.
Not only is it great for bonding, you'll also feel the benefits after
half an hour of chasing round the park.

### IN THE KITCHEN

Do a few bends and stretches by the sink (pretend
you're a ballerina at the barre) or dance around
the kitchen while you're waiting for the
kettle to boil.

**1** monthly goal

**2** weekly goal

**3** daily goal

**DATE**

| aerobic exercise | time | reps | other exercise | time | reps | progress |
|---|---|---|---|---|---|---|
| | | | | | | |

# index